D1558491

6/18

Pairs Skating

BY HEATHER E. SCHWARTZ

Consultant:
Kristin Eberth
United States Figure Skating double gold medalist
Professional figure skater with Disney On Ice

Snap Books are published by Capstone Press,
1710 Roe Crest Drive, North Mankato, Minnesota 56003
www.mycapstone.com

Library of Congress Cataloging-in-Publication Data
Names: Schwartz, Heather E., author.
Title: Pairs skating / By Heather Schwartz.
Description: North Mankato, Minnesota: Capstone Press, 2018. | Series: Snap
    Books. Figure Skating | Includes bibliographical references and index. |
    Audience: Age 8–9. | Audience: Grade 4 to 6.
Identifiers: LCCN 2017009728
ISBN 9781515781875 (library binding)
ISBN 9781515781912 (eBook PDF)
Subjects: LCSH: Pairs figure skating—Juvenile literature. | Figure
    skaters—Biography—Juvenile literature.
Classification: LCC GV850.4 .S385 2018 | DDC 796.91/2—dc23
LC record available at https://lccn.loc.gov/2017009728

Editorial Credits
Brenda Haugen, editor; Veronica Scott, designer; Kelli Lageson,
media researcher; Kathy McColley, production specialist

Photo Credits
Alamy: PA Images, 26, Tribune Content Agency, 9; Dreamstime: Eagleflying,
28; Getty Images: The LIFE Picture Collection/Mark Kauffman, 15 (bottom);
Newscom: Album, 25, FEATURECHINA/DEQIU SHA, 5, ZUMA Press/
TASS, 27, ZUMApress/H. Lorren Au Jr., 10; Shutterstock: anfisa focusova, 3,
Catalin Petolea, 22, Diego Barbieri, cover, Gertan, 24, Iurii Osadchi, 6, 7, 13, 23,
KPG_Payless, 11, LOFTFLOW, 8, Luca Santilli, 17, Olga Besnard, 12 (top and
bottom), 14, 15 (top), 18, 21, 29, Paolo Bona, 20, Shooter Bob Square Lenses,
cover, throughout, testing, 19

Design elements: Shutterstock

Printed and bound in Canada.
010395F17

Table of Contents

Pairs in Performance

As the music starts, a man and a woman glide over the ice. Their costumes shine in the spotlight as they skate, mirroring each other's movements. When the song picks up its tempo, the skaters speed up too. Their skates scrape the ice as they match their moves to the tune's dramatic notes. Each part of the program seems to bring the mood of the song to life.

The audience gasps at the pair's **synchronized** spins. They cheer when the pair performs a daring throw jump. They shout as the program ends with the skaters striking a pose.

Pairs skating is beautiful to watch. This form of figure skating can be fun to practice and perform too. Many skaters enjoy working closely with a partner. The support helps them each perfect their skills. It also helps them learn new ones. In pairs, skaters can go beyond anything they could do alone.

Fast Fact

Pairs skaters first competed at the Olympic Games in 1908.

4

synchronized—to perform movements at the same time

Chapter 1

Getting Started

Pairs skaters set their movements to music. They dazzle audiences with amazing jumps, lifts, spins, and throws. Their performances are unique in figure skating. Yet fans can't always tell the difference between pairs skating and other styles of figure skating.

Pairs skating is often confused with ice dancing. But only ice dancers are allowed to perform alone if they choose. Pairs skaters always need a partner. Pairs skaters face added challenges too. Their lifts are higher. Their programs must include difficult jumps, throws, **death spirals**, and spins that are not allowed in ice dancing.

Pairs skating includes breathtaking lifts.

Fast Fact

Ice dancing became an Olympic sport in 1976.

Pairs skating is actually more like singles skating than ice dancing. But pairs skaters have extra challenges to meet. They show many of the same skills as singles skaters. But they also have to include pairs **elements** in their programs, and they have to perform their skills at the same time.

death spiral—a move in which the male partner holds one hand of the female partner and rotates around a point, while the female partner rotates around him with her body parallel to the ice

element—a particular move in skating that has to be included in a competition or test routine

7

MAKING A MATCH

Figure skaters who want to skate in pairs can't go it alone. Each has to find a partner. Most skaters start the search by talking to their coaches. A coach might have someone in mind or at least be able to help. Web searches are another way to go. There are websites for skating partner searches.

Possible partners go through **tryouts**, which take place both on and off the ice. They skate together and show their skills and abilities. They also talk about their goals and how they might meet them together.

tryout—a test of someone's ability to see if he or she would make a good partner

Partners need to be able to talk honestly with each other.

Just the Facts

Skaters searching for a good pairs match often start by considering basic facts. Online listings include important information, such as competition level, age, height, location, and how to get in touch. Listings also allow skaters to say whether they will move to a new city to find a good match. None of this information tells skaters how well they will get along, of course. But it is a good place to start.

WORKING TOGETHER

Pairs skaters need to trust each other on the ice. Respect and good communication help build that trust. Pairs skaters share their goals to make sure they are on the same page. That helps them avoid problems while they are working together.

Pairs skaters often perform to music that's chosen for them. Their coach helps them learn **choreography** and perfect each element. If skaters choose their own music and plan choreography, both partners have to agree. They should both feel that their choices match their style, age, and abilities on the ice.

A good coach will guide you and help you improve.

ENDING A PARTNERSHIP

Sometimes pairs skaters find their partnership won't work. They don't have the same goals. They don't enjoy each other's company. They might even feel they don't trust and respect each other. If a pairs partnership feels uncomfortable to you, speak up. Tell your coach. He or she will help you find another partner.

Fast Fact

International skating rules changed to allow songs with words starting in 2014.

choreography—arrangement of steps, movements, and required elements that make up a pairs routine

Chapter 2

Pairs Moves

LIFTS

One of the moves pairs skating is known for is the lift. There are many lift styles.

Lasso Lift

The man swings his partner from one side of his body, around behind his head and into a raised position. Once in the lift, the female partner is in a split position facing the same direction as her partner.

lasso lift

star lift

Star Lift

The male partner raises his partner by her hip from his side into the air. Her legs are in a scissor position, with either one hand touching his shoulder or both hands free.

12

Tabletop Lift

The male partner lifts the female partner overhead with his hands on her hips. She is parallel to the ice with her arms stretched out to the sides.

Twist Lift

The male partner lifts the female partner overhead and tosses her in the air. She rotates in the air. The male partner catches her and puts her back on the ice.

twist lift

Fast Fact

The Lutz was named for skater Alois Lutz. He invented it as a jump style in 1913.

DEATH SPIRALS

Death spirals define pairs skating and excite crowds. It takes skill and practice to perform these moves with enough control to prevent a crash. Perfect form is impressive. It can result in high scores from judges during competitions. There are various types of death spirals, including:

Forward Inside Edge Death Spiral

In this version of the death spiral, the male partner skates on a backward outside edge of his skate. The female partner skates on a forward inside edge of her skate. The male partner performs a **pivot**, holding the hand of the female partner with his arm fully extended on the same side of his body as his skating foot. The female partner leans sideways to the ice with her arm also fully extended. She circles her male partner.

forward inside edge
death spiral

backward inside edge
death spiral

Backward Outside Edge Death Spiral

For this type of death spiral, both partners skate on a backward outside edge of their skates. The male partner performs a pivot, holding the hand of the female partner with his arm fully extended on the same side of his body as his skating foot. The female partner leans backward toward the ice with her arm also fully extended. She circles her male partner.

Fast Fact

Suzanne Morrow and Wallace Distelmeyer (right) performed the first death spiral at the 1948 Olympics.

pivot—to turn around a point

THROWS AND JUMPS

Pairs skaters also perform a variety of throws and jumps to impress judges and spectators. Following are a few of the crowd pleasers:

Pair Throw

The male partner assists his female partner as she launches from the ice into the air. She performs at least a half revolution and may perform multiple revolutions before landing.

Throw Toe Loop

The male partner assists as the female partner takes off from the back outside edge of her skating foot with assistance from the toe of her free foot. She rotates in the air and lands on the back outside edge of the opposite foot.

Salchow Jump

The male partner assists as the female partner takes off from the back inside edge of her skating foot. She rotates in the air and lands on the back outside edge of the opposite foot.

pair throw

Chapter 3

Getting Competitive

Competing in front of judges is part of the fun of pairs skating. Competitions give skaters goals to work toward. They also provide a big boost in confidence when skaters achieve high scores. Pairs skaters under age 14 start competing at the pre-juvenile level. They test and advance from there. They can continue competing at each level, advancing through the intermediate, novice, junior, and senior levels. Each level requires skaters to master more difficult skills.

Nicole Della Monica and Matteo Guarise of Italy perform at the European Skating Championship in 2015.

Only mixed gender pairs can compete at the highest levels. They must include one male skater and one female skater, according to the rules of the International Skating Union (ISU), which oversees the sport around the world. Senior-level pairs skaters compete by performing a short program and then a long program. The short program is no more than 2 minutes and 40 seconds long, plus or minus 10 seconds. The long program is 4 minutes and 30 seconds, plus or minus 10 seconds. Each program must include certain elements, such as lifts and jumps.

Get the Look

Pairs skaters practice in clothing that moves with them and doesn't get in the way. Form-fitting clothing allows the coach to better see the skaters' body positions and make corrections. At competitions, pairs skaters wear costumes that reflect the themes of their programs. There are strict rules about what kinds of costumes skaters can wear, but ISU rules allow clothing

that matches the character of the skaters' music. Breaking the rules can result in lost points, but many pairs skaters take the risk. Points are rarely taken away for costume choices.

SKATING FOR SCORES

Pairs skaters want to create a program that will impress the judges. Judges look for required moves throughout the program. They score performances based partly on the following criteria.

Judges watch for many things during a performance, including required elements.

Death Spirals

The male skater must be in full pivot position. While the female skater's head must be close to the ice, it must not touch the ice. She may not use any part of her body to assist herself.

Lifts

Skaters must perform a complete lift with the male partner's arm fully extended. The male partner must perform a minimum number of revolutions depending on the skating level.

Jumps

Skaters must perform solo jumps, jump combinations, and jump sequences.

Spins

Skaters must perform a minimum number of revolutions based on their level. They must rotate at least three times for it to count as a spin.

Step Sequence

Skaters must complete one step sequence that covers from half the ice surface to the entire ice sheet, depending on their test level.

Throw Jumps

Skaters must perform throw jumps in which the female partner is thrown into the air by the male partner and lands unassisted on a backward outside edge of one of her skates.

Twist Lifts

Skaters must perform twist lifts in which the male partner catches the female partner in the air and assists her landing.

Chapter 4

Best of the Best

Pairs skaters spend a lot of time practicing. It's the only way to make it to the highest levels of competition at the U.S. National Championships, the World Championships, and the Olympics. Skaters are on the ice for several hours each day. They work with a coach who can help them perfect their skills. They practice their moves, including lifts, throws, and spins. And they train to gain speed and **agility**.

Training for pairs skating also includes plenty of work off the ice. Pairs skaters hit the gym for exercises that will build better balance, agility, power, and strength. In addition to working out, they have to eat right and get enough sleep. The best diet for an **elite** pairs skater includes plenty of lean protein and little to no junk food.

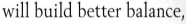

agility—the ability to move quickly and easily

elite—among the best

Skaters' muscles get hard workouts during performances. A good night's sleep helps skaters' muscles recover.

Super Sleepers

At the U.S. Olympic Complex in Colorado Springs, Colorado, an expert helped set up rooms so athletes can get a great night's rest. Skaters sleep in cool rooms with sound machines or fans to block out noise. There's just enough light for them to see if they get up in the night. They have alarm clocks to help them wake up. The goal is about eight hours of sleep each night. Sleep gives skaters' bodies time to restore muscles, so they can perform their very best.

Fast Fact

Early ice skates had blades made of bone or wood. Steel blades were invented around 1850.

UNDER PRESSURE

Elite pairs skaters are at the top of their game. But that does not mean they don't feel stress before they perform. In fact, skating at the highest levels can mean even more anxiety. These skaters enter competitions where the whole world is watching. They have a lot to lose if they make a mistake. Still, they hold their nerves in check. How? By managing and reducing their anxiety. Skaters prepare for competition-day stress with even more training. They practice their programs mentally when they're not on the ice. They memorize them and walk through them without performing all of the moves. They even teach themselves to feel anxiety and release it.

Vanessa James and Morgan Cipres of France skate during an official practice at the ISU World Figure Skating Championships.

Any stress that's left is put to use on the ice. Pairs skaters let their stress help them improve during practice. A racing heart and a rush of adrenaline signal more than panic to a pairs skater. They are physical signals that help pairs skaters focus and energize their performance.

Fast Fact

At her first Olympic Games, in 1924, Sonia Henie (right) was so stressed she stopped and asked her coach for help during her routine. She later won three Olympic gold medals.

Chapter 5

Pairs Figure Skating Legends

MADGE AND EDGAR SYERS

Madge Cave was already a figure skater when she met her new coach, Edgar Syers, in 1899. He coached her in the new skating style of the late 1800s. They eventually married and started skating both solo and together.

Madge broke many barriers for women in figure skating. In 1902 she became the first woman to skate in the World Championships. In 1906 and 1908, she won the women's World Championship title. She also made popular a shorter skirt style for female skaters. The new style allowed judges to see the women's feet while they skated.

Madge won the first Olympic gold medal awarded for women's figure skating at the 1908 Games. The same year, she and Edgar skated for Great Britain and won an Olympic bronze medal in pairs.

EKATERINA GORDEEVA AND SERGEI GRINKOV

Russian skaters Ekaterina Gordeeva and Sergei Grinkov started skating together as teenagers. They performed well, winning the European Championships, the World Championships, and other major competitions. In 1988 they skated in the Olympics and won a gold medal. Ekaterina was 16 years old. Sergei was 21.

As they grew up, the pair fell in love. They married in 1991. They continued skating together and went to the 1994 Olympics. They won another gold medal.

The couple was training together when tragedy struck. Sergei had a heart attack on the ice. He died in 1995 at age 28. Ekaterina has continued skating solo.

SHEN XUE AND ZHAO HONGBO

Chinese skaters Shen Xue and Zhao Hongbo began their partnership on the ice in 1992. They won many competitions, including three World Championships. Their relationship grew as they trained and competed. Zhao proposed to Shen after the 2007 World Championships. They were married in a private ceremony later that year.

The couple retired from skating for two years but returned for the Olympics. They won an Olympic gold medal in pairs in 2010. It was China's first Olympic gold medal in figure skating.

A few months later, they celebrated with a public marriage ceremony on the ice in China. Thousands of fans witnessed the event. The pair has retired from skating but continues to promote their sport.

ALIONA SAVCHENKO AND ROBIN SZOLKOWY

German pair Aliona Savchenko and Robin Szolkowy teamed up in 2003. They won five World Championships. They also won bronze medals at the 2010 and 2014 Olympics. After the 2014 Olympics, Robin decided to retire from skating. He did not feel his body was up to the challenge anymore. Aliona chose to continue. She found a new partner, French skater Bruno Massot. Together they began training to skate in the 2018 Olympic Games.

Aliona Savchenko
and Robin Szolkowy

Glossary

adrenaline (uh-DREH-nuh-luhn)—a substance that is released in the body causing the heart to beat faster and giving more energy

agility (uh-GI-luh-tee)—the ability to move quickly and easily

anxiety (ang-ZYE-uh-tee)—a feeling of worry or fear

choreography (kor-ee-OG-ruh-fee)—arrangement of steps, movements, and required elements that make up a pairs routine

death spiral (DETH SPI-ruhl)—a move in which the male partner holds one hand of the female partner and rotates around a point, while the female partner rotates around him with her body parallel to the ice

element (EL-uh-muhnt)—a particular move in skating that has to be included in a competition or test routine

elite (i-LEET)—among the best

pivot (PIH-vut)—to turn around a point

protein (PRO-teen)—a substance found in foods such as meat, milk, eggs, and beans that is an important part of the human diet

revolution (rev-uh-LOO-shuhn)—circular movement

sychnronized (SING-kruh-nyzd)—to perform movements at the same time

tempo (TEM-poh)—the speed of a song

tryout (TRY-owt)—a test of someone's ability to see if he or she would make a good partner

Read More

Jamrosz, Joanne. *Skating with the World*. Concord, North Carolina: Comfort Publishing, 2014.

Waxman, Laura Hamilton. *Winter Olympic Sports: Figure Skating*. Mankato, Minnesota: Amicus Ink, 2017.

Wood, Alex. *You Can Be an Ice Skater*. Milwaukee, Wisconsin: Gareth Stevens Publishing, 2014.

Internet Sites

Use FactHound to find Internet sites related to this book.

Visit *www.facthound.com*

Just type in 9781515781875 and go.

 Check out projects, games and lots more at
www.capstonekids.com

Index